Wh [illegible] ea so salty?

FOX EYE
PUBLISHING

Why is the sea salty?

Because it has lots
of mineral ions in it.

Why is it full of mineral ions?

Because the mineral ions come from the rivers that flow into the sea.

Why do they come from the rivers?

Because they are in the rainwater that flows off the land into the rivers.

Why are they in the rainwater?

Because the rainwater
has picked them up
from rocks on the
high ground and in
the mountains.

So why aren't rivers salty?

Rivers are always washing the ions down to the sea. There are so many mineral ions now trapped in sea, you can taste some of them.

Let's find out about sea water.

Turn the page over to discover the answers to these questions.

Can you drink sea water?
How do you make sea salt?
How big is the sea?

Let's find out about sea water.

The answers are ...

Mineral ions are very, very, tiny, electrically charged, pieces of rock.

Mostly water and Sodium and Chloride mineral ions.

There are about 6 teaspoons of salt in a litre of sea water.

No. It has too much salt in it for your body to process.
Heat up some sea water until it has all evaporated, leaving behind tiny white crystals of salt.
70% of the surface of the world is covered by sea water. That is more than double the amount of land.

How to use this book

You can read this book with one child or a group of children.

The book can be used to begin a discussion around complex questions such as learning why the sea is so salty.

The book is also a reading aid, with enlarged and repeated words to help children to develop their reading skills.

How to read the story

Before beginning the story, ensure that the children you are reading to are relaxed and focused.

Take time to look at the enlarged words and the illustrations, and discuss what this book might be about before reading the story.

New words can be tricky for young children to approach.

Sounding them out first, slowly and repeatedly, can help children to learn the words and become familiar with them.

Did you spot
the Tardigrade
hiding in
this book?

First published in 2023 by Fox Eye Publishing
Unit 31, Vulcan House Business Centre,
Vulcan Road, Leicester, LE5 3EF
www.foxeyepublishing.com

Written and illustrated by Simon Couchman

ISBN 978-1-80445-359-9

A catalogue record for this book is available from the British Library.

Printed in China

Titles in the Series

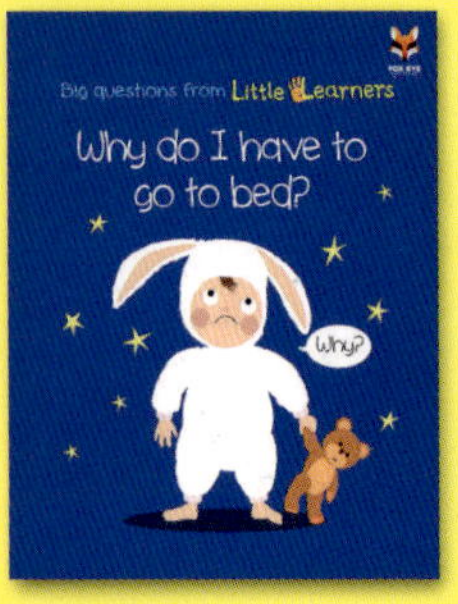

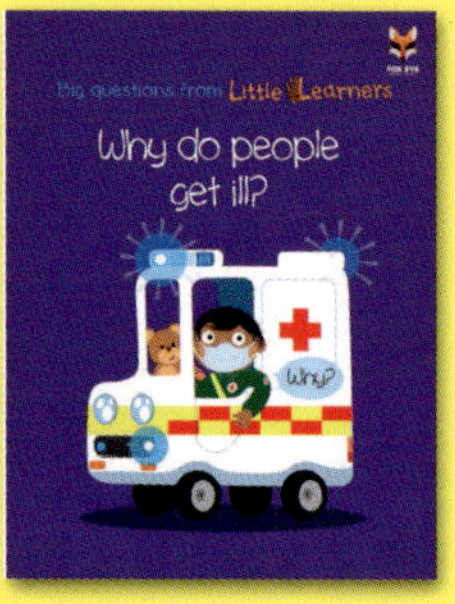

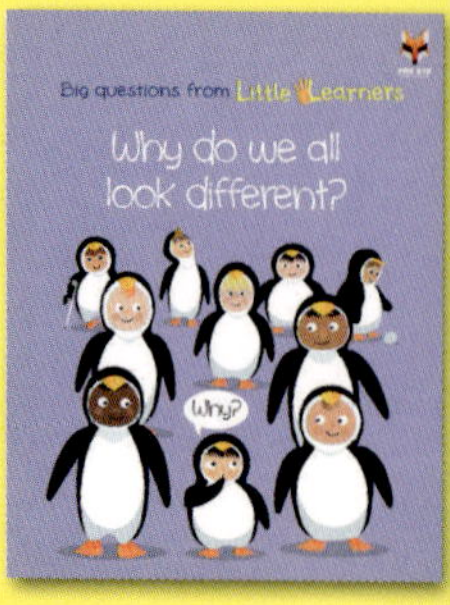

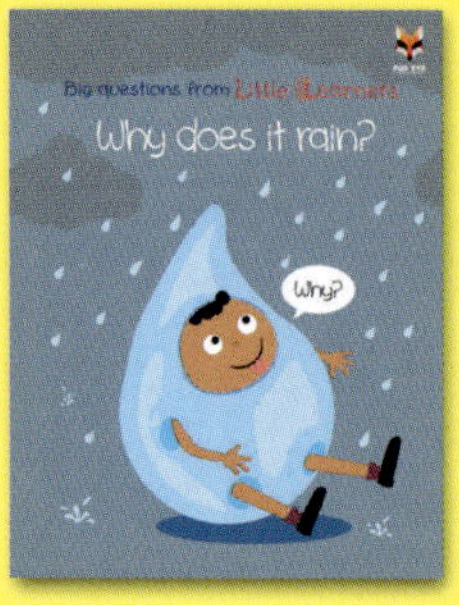

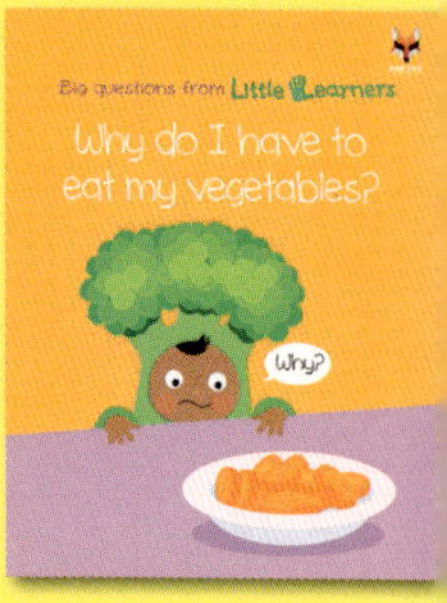